Tomorrow's World

The COMPUTERIZED SOCIETY

Steve Pizzey & Sheila Snowden

The Bookwright Press
New York · 1986

Tomorrow's World

Our Future in Space
The Telecommunications Revolution
Lasers in Action
The Robot Age
The Computerized Society
Living in the Future

First published in the United States in 1986 by
The Bookwright Press
387 Park Avenue South
New York, NY 1006

First published in 1985 by Wayland (Publishers) Limited
61 Western Road, Hove, East Sussex BN3 1JD, England
© 1985 Wayland (Publishers) Limited

ISBN 0–531–18039–5
Library of Congress Catalog Card Number 85–62083

Phototypeset by Kalligraphics Ltd., Redhill, Surrey
Printed in Italy by G. Canale & C.S.p.A., Turin, Italy

Contents

2284802

The computer revolution 4

The information explosion 9

Computers in control 18

The computer industry 23

Communicating with the machine 28

Leisure and learning 33

Artificial intelligence 41

Glossary 46
Further reading 46
Index 47

The computer revolution

Whether we like it or not, much of the way we live today depends on computers behind the scenes. Computers are lurking in gas stations, keeping the pumps under control and adding up the cost. They are creeping into the telephone networks, quietly switching millions of phone calls. They are also hiding in video cassette players linking the controls to the electronics, in supermarkets adding up totals – and, as everyone knows, they are always sending us bills!

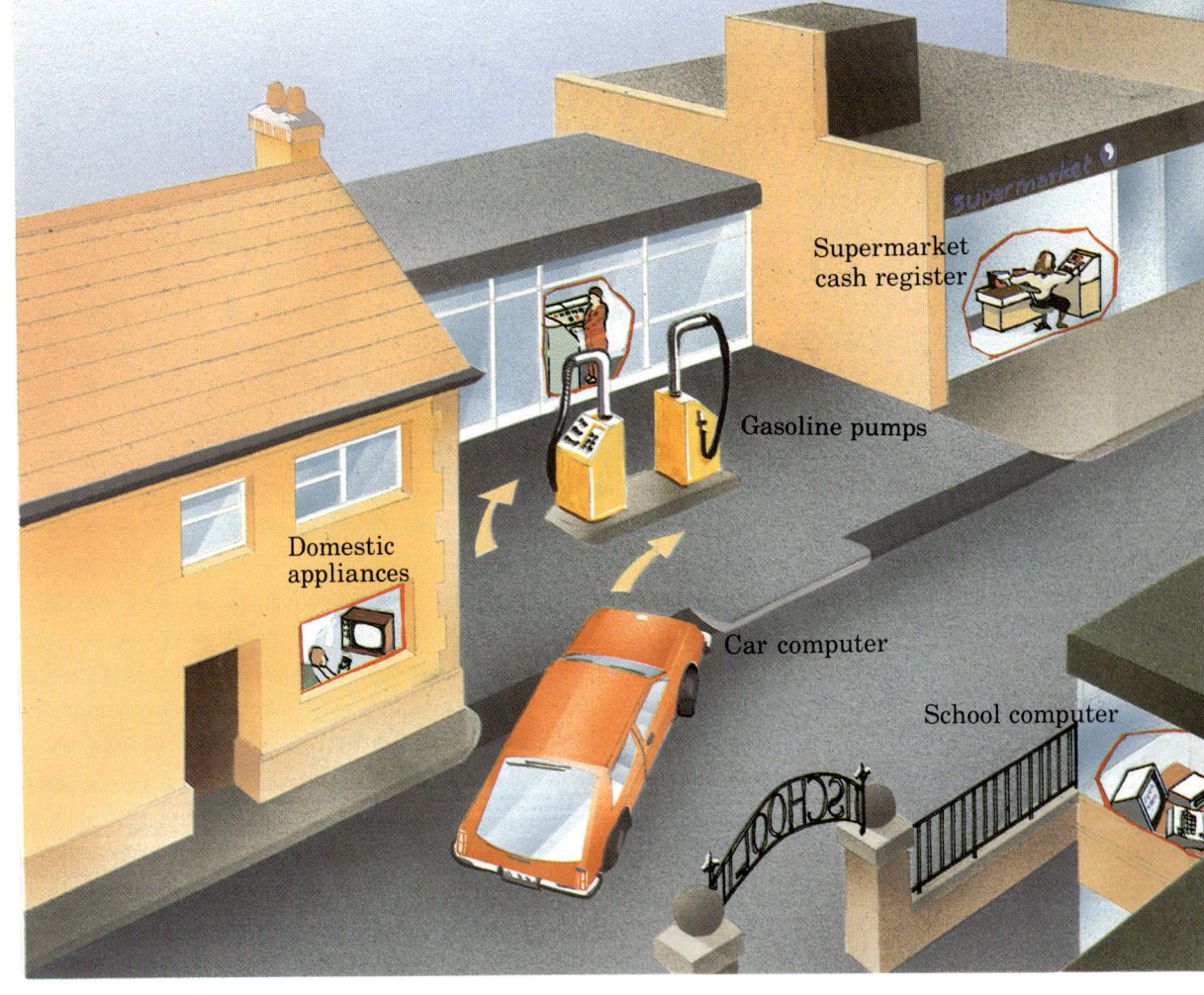

Supermarket cash register

Gasoline pumps

Domestic appliances

Car computer

School computer

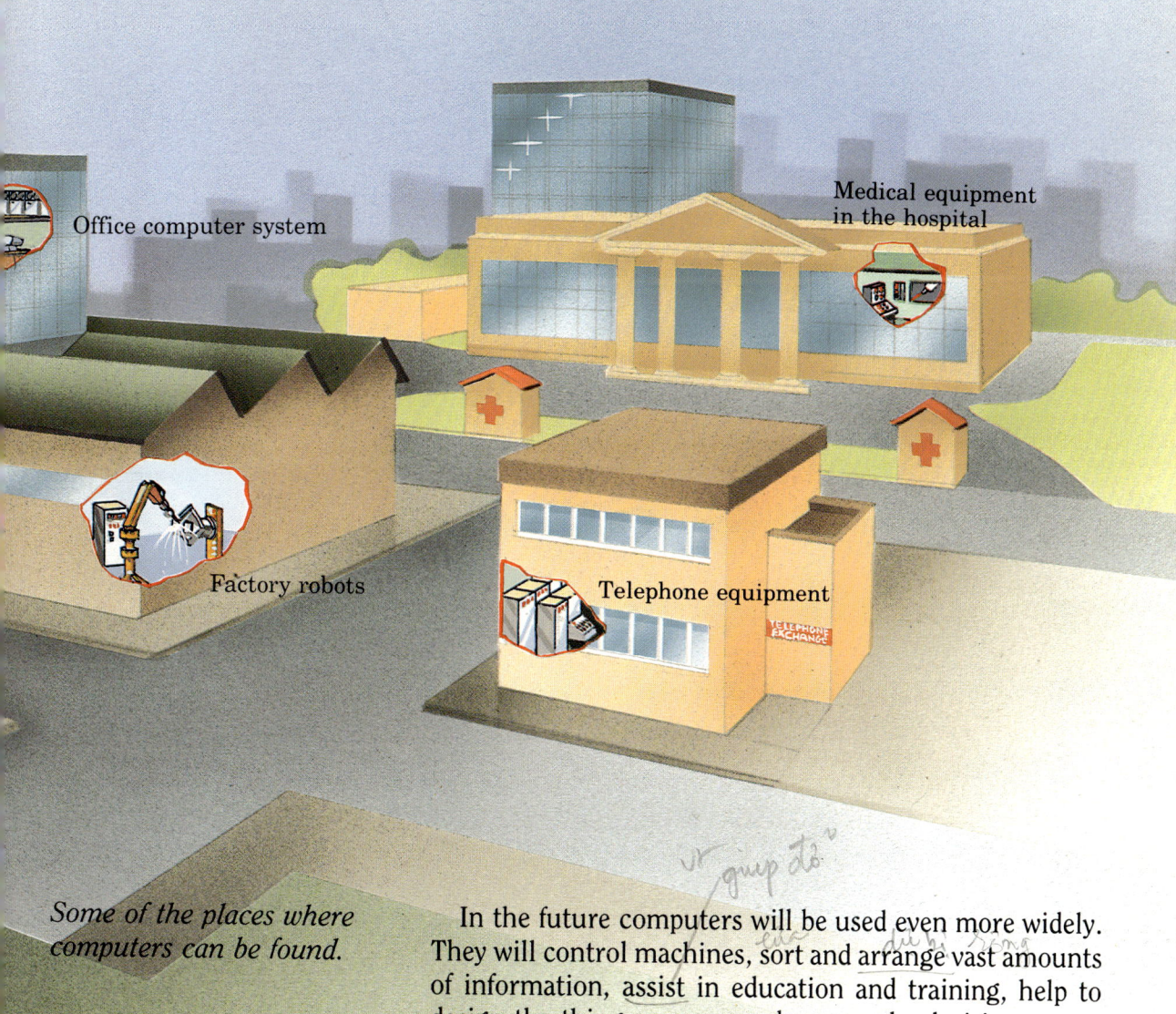

Some of the places where computers can be found.

In the future computers will be used even more widely. They will control machines, sort and arrange vast amounts of information, assist in education and training, help to design the things we use, and even make decisions.

What is a computer?

How does a computer differ from any other machine, such as a can opener or an airplane? Basically, the answer is that a computer is not one machine, but many. A can opener can only be used to open cans; an airplane can only transport passengers or freight. There is no way you can change a can opener or an airplane into something else without totally rebuilding it.

But a computer can be programmed to perform completely different tasks. So, identical computers can be used to control other machines, or sort information, even to play games, without being rebuilt or changed in any way at all. The computer program is simply a set of instructions to turn the computer into a new machine.

Just as humans can learn all sorts of varied tasks (such as playing chess, or fixing cars) so computers can be programmed to perform in many different ways. This is at the heart of the computer revolution and this is why the computer is finding its way into so many areas of our lives.

Inside a busy computer room. Large computers can store huge amounts of information.

What can computers do?

The incredible speed at which computers work means they can carry out calculations that would take a person years or even centuries to work out. In fact this is how the first computers were used – as giant calculators. Colossus, one of the world's first electronic computers, was built in Britain during World War II. It was used to crack German secret codes by carrying out many thousands of repetitive calculations quickly.

Computers can also sort information and store it in electronic form. They do this so well that in the year 2000 there may be no such thing as offices full of pieces of paper stored in filing cabinets. Instead, the information will be tucked away on magnetic disks or some form of super memory chip.

A computer picture of a car (above), and the finished car.

Computer-aided design

Computers are now used to design equipment and prepare plans. Computer-aided design (CAD) is used in industry to design such things as cars, aircraft, even computers themselves. This type of program is now available in a limited way for home computers.

Imagine you wanted to design your own car, for example. Having drawn in the basic shape you could ask the computer to show you how it would look from any angle, without your having to draw it over and over again. Each separate part of the car could be designed in this way.

Copying, or simulating, the world is another use for computers. Large, computer-controlled aircraft simulators are used to train pilots, and simple flight simulator programs are available for home computers. The advantage of learning to fly a jumbo jet by computer is obvious – crashing real planes is dangerous and expensive! It is better to learn on a flight simulator first, where all sorts of hazardous situations, too risky to try out on a real aircraft, can be tested.

Computers are also helping to train mechanics and engineers, as well as pilots. They will become even more useful when linked to video or cassettes, since the computer will then be able to call on real photographs and movie film to help the trainees.

Today we accept that computers handle large amounts of information, print out lists and are generally involved in the daily running of businesses. Tomorrow we shall see computers involved in a more creative way, actually designing objects and creating ideas.

Inside the cockpit of a Boeing 747 jumbo jet. Pilots are trained to fly large aircraft in computer-controlled flight simulators.

The information explosion

We are constantly taking in all kinds of information through our senses – for example, what time the next bus leaves, what programs are on TV, what someone is saying to us, what we are reading, what we can see from the window.

The amount of information available today is far greater than at any other time in history, and it is increasing all the time. This is what is called the "information explosion." Even your local newsstand contains more magazines and newspapers than you could possibly read before they became out of date.

Many people use computers at home to play games, to remind them of dates such as birthdays and when to pay the bills or, as here, to store recipes.

What is information?

Information can appear in various ways: as printed words, as images on a TV screen, as a diagram, or as something you yourself can draw or tell someone. To give information to someone, you do not actually need to make anything: you simply decide what you want to tell the person, then either say it, write it, draw it, telephone it or type it.

The computer is especially useful for organizing information. It can store an enormous amount of information and it will sort it out, reorganize it or let you search for something as you wish. It can then present the information on a screen, or print it out on paper, or send it as electronic signals along a wire to another computer.

It is now possible to type in a letter on your home computer, link it to a telephone and send the message over the telephone so it appears on your friend's computer screen. In the future, electronic mail will be an important method of communication, as it is much faster than sending letters. Large industrial companies and governments already send information in this way all the time.

A businessman proudly showing off the computer that has been fitted into his chauffeur-driven limousine.

Word processing

Reducing the enormous variety of information to a series of numbers inside the computer means that information can be handled much more easily. Word processor programs make it possible to use a computer for writing and editing the written word.

The words are entered on the keyboard, as they are on a typewriter, but they appear on the computer's screen, not on paper. At the touch of a few keys you can alter words on the screen, correct errors or shift sentences around until you are satisfied with them. You can also copy pieces of text, so that you do not have to type the same thing over and over again. You can then print the whole thing out.

This is quicker and easier than changing and correcting words on paper, which is messy and time-consuming. Soon typewriters will be as outdated as old radiograms are today.

A cashless society?

Computers are also making it possible for us to have a "cashless society," in which paper money and coins may disappear altogether in the future. In many cases today, money is transferred simply by sending information from one company's computer to another's. There is very rarely

With a word processor program, a computer can deal with all the typing jobs done in an office.

any need to handle real money at all. If your salary appears only as a number on your paycheck, and you pay for everything you buy with a credit card, and then pay off the credit card bill by check, you need handle no cash at all.

Databases

Large amounts of information are stored in databases. These are the electronic equivalent of filing cabinets and libraries, with the information being stored in a computer and not on paper. Some computers exist solely to store and organize the vast amount of information that people now have to deal with. The information has to be fed into the computer in the first place, of course, but once there the information can be retrieved very quickly. Any record or fact can be found and displayed on a screen almost instantaneously.

The advantages are enormous. Whereas information on paper can be arranged in only one order – say alphabetically by surname – the computer can keep rearranging the data in whichever way is required. For example, in a hospital, doctors might prefer to organize the records differently according to a patient's age, or the type of illness, or the number of days spent in hospital. Using a computer system, doctors can quickly gather statistics about many different illnesses to help them in their research. Without a computer they would have to read through every paper record.

Large organizations

Databases are ideal for organizations that handle large amounts of information, such as travel agencies, universities, libraries, and so on. One large computer generally holds the database, and this central store of information can be called up over the telephone system by small computers anywhere in the country. For a travel agent, the latest travel information can be called up on the screen.

Databases store large amounts of information, especially for businesses and public organizations.

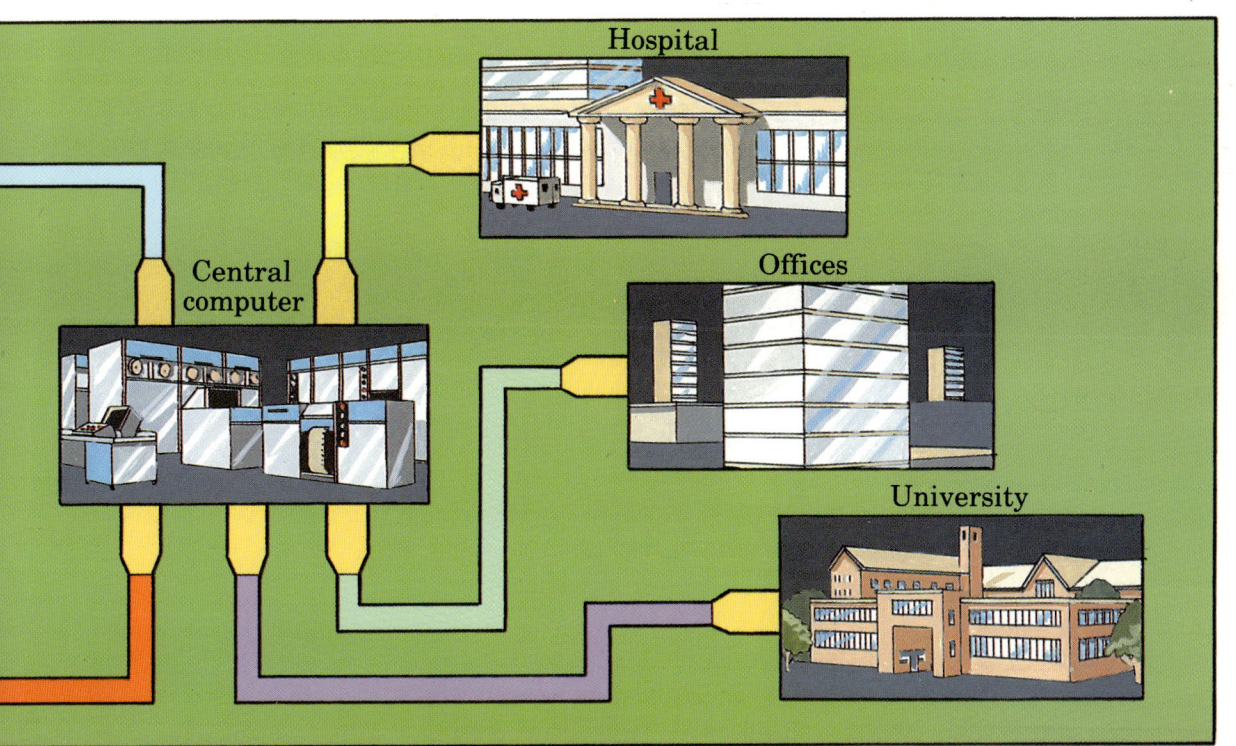

When a vacation trip is booked, the details are fed back to the main computer and the database is updated. Universities and researchers can call on databases containing whole libraries and encyclopedias. Electronic "bulletin boards" for exchanging data are available to anyone with a telephone, a home computer and a modem (a device to link a computer to the telephone).

This Londoner is using a modem (the black device next to the computer) to call up a British database called Prestel over the telephone system.

Personal files

Personal information, too, is held on computer files. Banks, doctors, police, the Internal Revenue Service, all store their records in this way. The police computer holds details of criminal records and car registration documents. A policeman, while on his beat, can call up the main computer and check on a car license plate to see if it has been stolen, or check on someone's name to see if that person has a criminal record, or is known to the police. As a result there is a greater chance of catching criminals.

Banks have the details of each account on their computer, and this allows automatic money-dispensing machines to check a customer's balance, pay out money and debit his or her account, without any paperwork or human effort being involved.

Are databases dangerous?

Most people agree that databases are generally a good thing. But many people are also concerned about the amount of personal information that is stored in this way. They are afraid that it could get into the wrong hands. For instance, when applying for a job you may not feel it necessary for your future employer to know about a long illness you had in the past. And, even if you feel you have nothing to hide, you may not want details of your bank account to get into the hands of loan companies. Bank records show the exact time and place any transactions occur. While a criminal will obviously want to keep this information quiet, law-abiding citizens who have done nothing wrong may also prefer privacy, even from the police.

The Internal Revenue Service (IRS) computer center in West Virginia. Computer databanks contain the personal details of millions of people.

Computer databases are widely used by the police, and by companies and government departments all over the world.

Right *Inside the foreign exchange department of a bank. Computers are needed to store up-to-the-minute information about financial transactions.*

The records held in the database may also contain incorrect or misleading information. In the United States, everyone has the right to look at his or her own records, but in some countries, such as Britain, this is not the case. In fact you cannot even find out if a record is held on you, let alone check whether the information in it is correct or not. And what would happen if such records were stolen?

Computer crime

Even if you are sure that the organizations in control of the computers have your best interests at heart, it is very difficult to make the information secure. The data are usually protected by a series of passwords that the user has to type in. But computer crime is on the increase, and such codewords can be bypassed. There is danger that private information could be stolen or tampered with without anyone's finding out.

Computers in control

Computers already control gasoline pumps, cruise missiles, spacecraft, airplanes, industrial machines, washing machines and video players. In the future, many more machines will contain small computers to control them.

Computers in factories
In engineering, complicated shapes can be cut out of metal using computer-controlled lathes and drilling machines. In some industries there are factories containing more than one hundred machines, all controlled by computer. The computers are kept nearby in air-conditioned rooms and linked to the machines by wires. These factories make complicated components for the aircraft industry. However, the computers can be reprogrammed to make many other shapes using the same machines.

Computers in transport
Computers also play an important part in controlling aircraft by monitoring fuel consumption, airspeed and altitude. Many aircraft can take off, fly and land using only the computer-controlled automatic pilot system, although usually the human pilot takes over for takeoff and landing. On the Concorde, computers control the amount of fuel in the various fuel tanks in the wings. As fuel is used up by the engines, the remainder is pumped from one tank to another to keep the plane balanced in flight.

There are railroads in Japan where computers are used to control the distance between trains, to get the maximum use out of the track while avoiding collisions.

Computer controls in the home
The invention of the microprocessor chip has made it possible to put a small computer into many ordinary machines, such as washing machines or central-heating controllers.

Space Shuttle flights are controlled by computer from takeoff to touchdown.

The microprocessor is at the heart of the computer, processing all the instructions, while the instructions themselves are stored on other chips, called memory chips.

There are also chips with both the processor and the memory built into them. These chips need sensors, such as temperature sensors, to tell them what is going on. A washing machine controller, for example, will need one

Just some of the everyday devices that are controlled by microprocessor chips.

sensor to detect how much water is in the machine, and another to check the temperature. The microprocessor then switches on heaters, valves, pumps and motors according to the program stored in its memory and selected by the user. Now that chips are mass-produced and no longer expensive, it is cheaper to control machines by electronics than by gear wheels and levers.

In all of these cases the computer is able to make continuous, fine adjustments far more quickly than a human could. So an aircraft or a train or a washing machine can be made much more efficient, saving both time and money and getting the most from the machine. The future will inevitably see electronics being used in machines of all types.

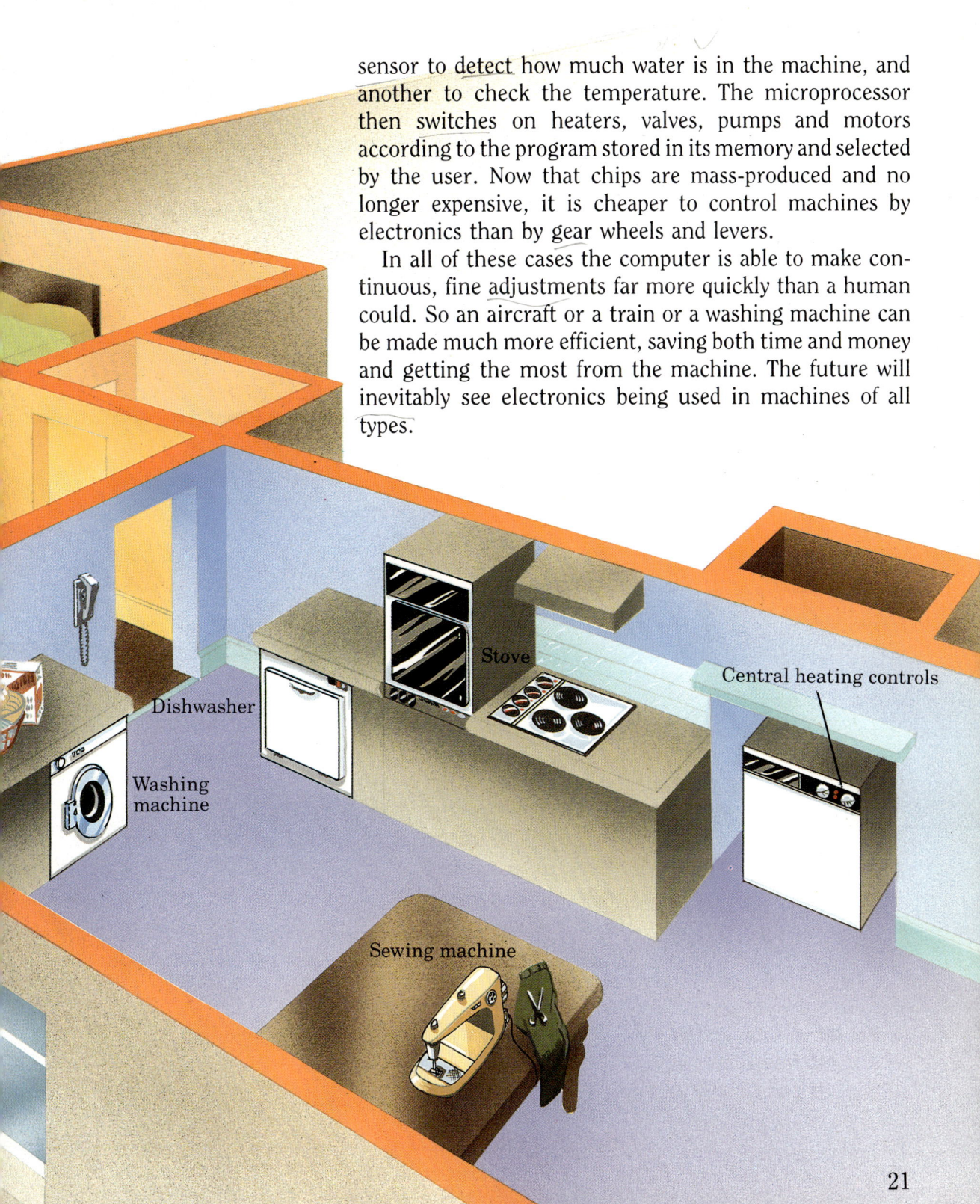

A robot being "taught" how to perform a task.

Robots

Robots are usually thought of as quite different from other types of machines, but really they are just mechanical devices controlled by a computer, like many other machines. The difference lies in the fact that robots are more versatile. Like computers, they can be programmed to carry out a variety of tasks. For example, identical robot arms can be programmed to spray a car with paint, or drill a hole, or move boxes of equipment, whereas most ordinary machines are built to carry out only one task.

Today's robots are fairly limited in what they can do. However, the robots of the future will have sophisticated computer controls and be fitted with sensors enabling them to see and find their way round. They will also be more intelligent and capable of making simple decisions about the best way to tackle a job.

The computer industry

In 1893 Henry Ford designed his first "gasoline buggy," and thus started the car industry which has helped shape the modern world. Building cars, making roads and everything else to do with the car, created new industries unimagined before. Today, less than a century later, half the gross domestic production of Europe is due to new industries undreamed of in Henry Ford's day.

The production of computers and software (programs), along with their introduction into our working and leisure

A circuit board from a computer is being tested.

activities, has been called the new industrial revolution. Many traditional industries are closing down, causing social hardship and unemployment, while new computer industries are springing up, often in different parts of the country, and providing work for others.

Above *The first computers were huge machines, needing a large room to themselves and a staff of people to look after them.*

The first computers

In 1943 the first electronic computer was built in Britain. It was constructed in secret and designed to crack German codes during the World War II. This machine, called Colossus, used large electronic valves, since transistors and chips had not been invented.

General-purpose computers started to be built in the 1950s and began to be used by industry. By 1958 there were 2,500 computers in the world, each costing thousands of dollars. By 1978 there were half a million computers in use worldwide and now there are millions of home computers in the United States alone.

The new industry

No other industry in history has grown so fast and demanded so many new skills. There is widespread unemployment in other industries, and yet there is a huge demand for people to write computer programs. The future will tell whether our society can cope with these problems.

Right *Silicon chips are tested with probes to see that they work properly before they are sealed in their own plastic cases. The inset shows a close-up of a chip.*

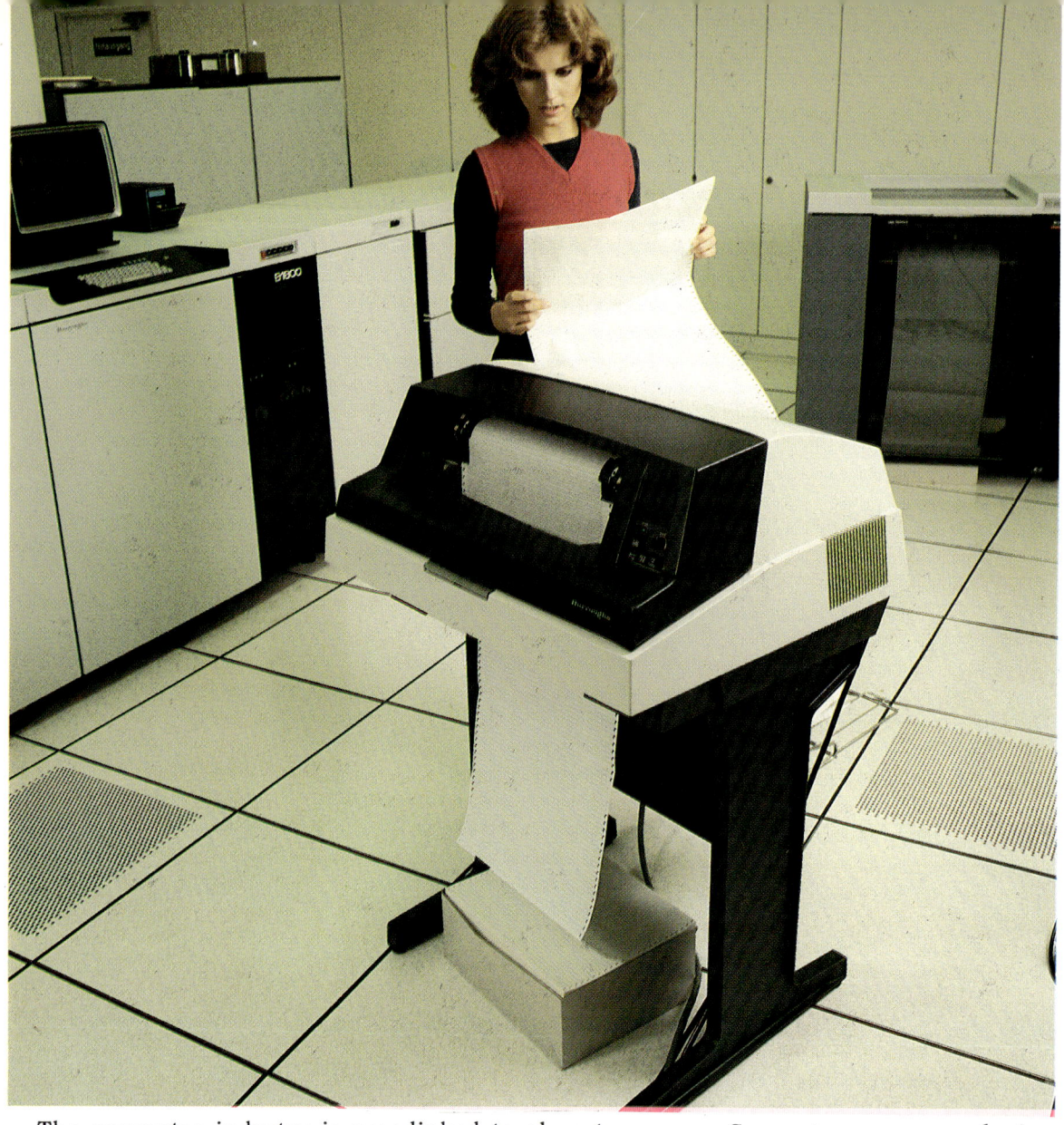

The computer industry is now linked to almost every other industry, since computers assist in designing products, ordering materials, managing companies and running businesses. This does not mean that humans will not be needed. Human judgment, skill, inventiveness and concern for others are far more valuable than any computer. What has happened is that computers have become accepted as tools and components of the modern age, almost as wrenches and nuts and bolts are used in simple engineering.

Computers are now playing an important part in industry – from the design and testing of new products to the delivery of goods to customers.

New inventions in electronics

The growth of the computer industry could not have taken place without inventions in electronics. The transistor was invented in 1948, and the chip, which consists of many hundreds of transistors on a small piece of silicon, was developed in the 1960s. Only with the chip was it possible to make cheaper, smaller and more powerful computers. Nowadays it is possible to put a million electronic components on one small chip of silicon the size of a fingernail. In many ways the industry is waiting for the software to catch up with the technology.

The future will see a new generation of computers which will be easier to use and capable of solving problems and making decisions. These will use the latest chip technology, new computer languages and artificial intelligence as well. The design of these computers is based on new ideas in the theory of computing, as well as the latest technology.

Computers were made possible by technological advances, but now it is computers which are bringing about new advances.

Communicating with the machine

Nowadays most data are fed into computers through keyboards of various kinds. In the future, contact could be even more direct, with voice recognition and speech synthesis. This would enable someone simply to talk to the computer, giving it information. The computer would then process this spoken information and reply in its own "voice." Many of the problems involved in creating an acceptable voice have now been sorted out. There are even computers with friendly voices!

There are many ways in which computers can take in information. Keyboards are common and likely to remain so. Keyboards that double as cash registers are likely to become more commonly used in stores, for they automatically store information about the product being sold and send data to a computer dealing with stock control. This enables the storekeeper to know exactly what stock the store has and which goods need reordering.

What you type into the computer depends on the language it has been designed to accept. The computer itself uses machine code – a language consisting only of small electronic pulses representing "on" or "off," or 0 and 1. Early programmers had to program computers in machine code, but this was so difficult that intermediate languages, closer to English, were soon invented. The computer translates these new words into its own machine code before carrying out the instructions.

The most popular language for home computers is BASIC (Beginner's All-purpose Symbolic Instruction Code). This is quite close to English and most people find it fairly easy to use.

There are many other languages. Some are designed to use words and symbols familiar to engineers or accountants or other business people. All these languages have to be very precise. A misplaced comma or period can prevent a

Keyboards are common tools for feeding data into computers.

program from running. The trend now is to make languages more "user friendly" by using methods and words familiar to everybody, and to make them more tolerant of our mistakes.

Sensors

Typing words and symbols on a keyboard is not the only way we can communicate with the computer. Computers will also take information directly from sensors fitted to machines. These sensors measure such things as temperature or light level, or detect movement.

Pictures can also be fed in from an electronic eye in the form of a camera. The future is likely to see more information fed into computers in this way, as computer memories are now big enough and cheap enough to store all the information contained in a picture.

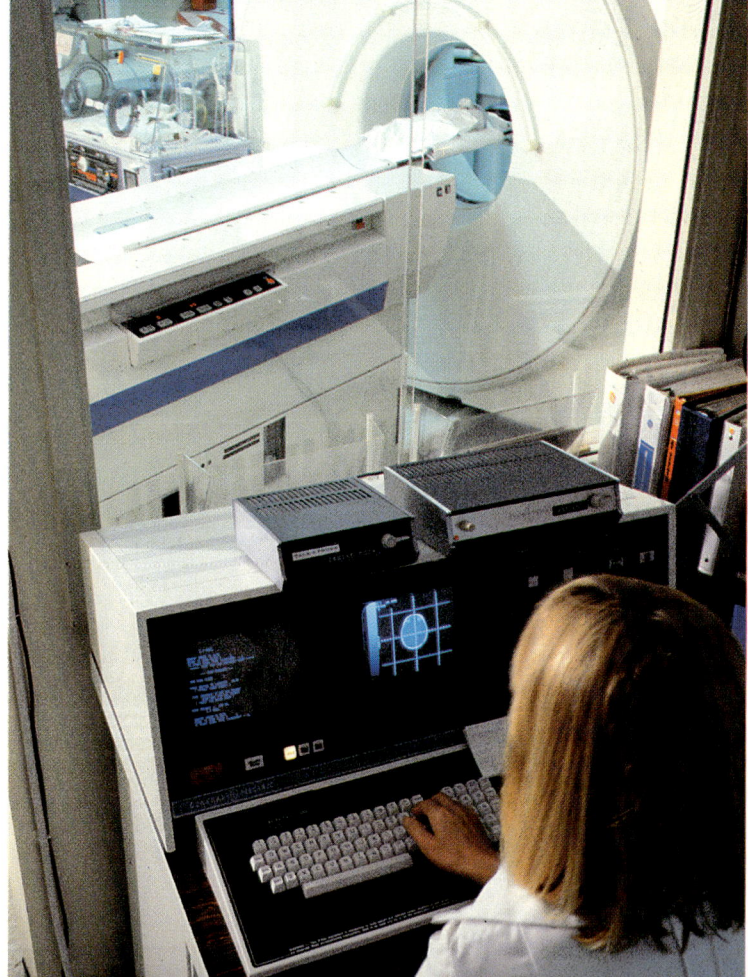

Computers are used to control the most up-to-date medical equipment such as this X-ray scanner.

Light pens and touch screens

Light pens and touch screens can also be used to input information. These are usually used to select one of several options displayed on the screen. You simply move the light pen to the option you wish to select, or point your finger to it on the touch screen. The light pen detects its position by timing the scanning electron beam that makes up the display on the monitor. The touch screen consists of a crisscross of fine wires that respond when you touch them with your finger.

A touch screen in use.

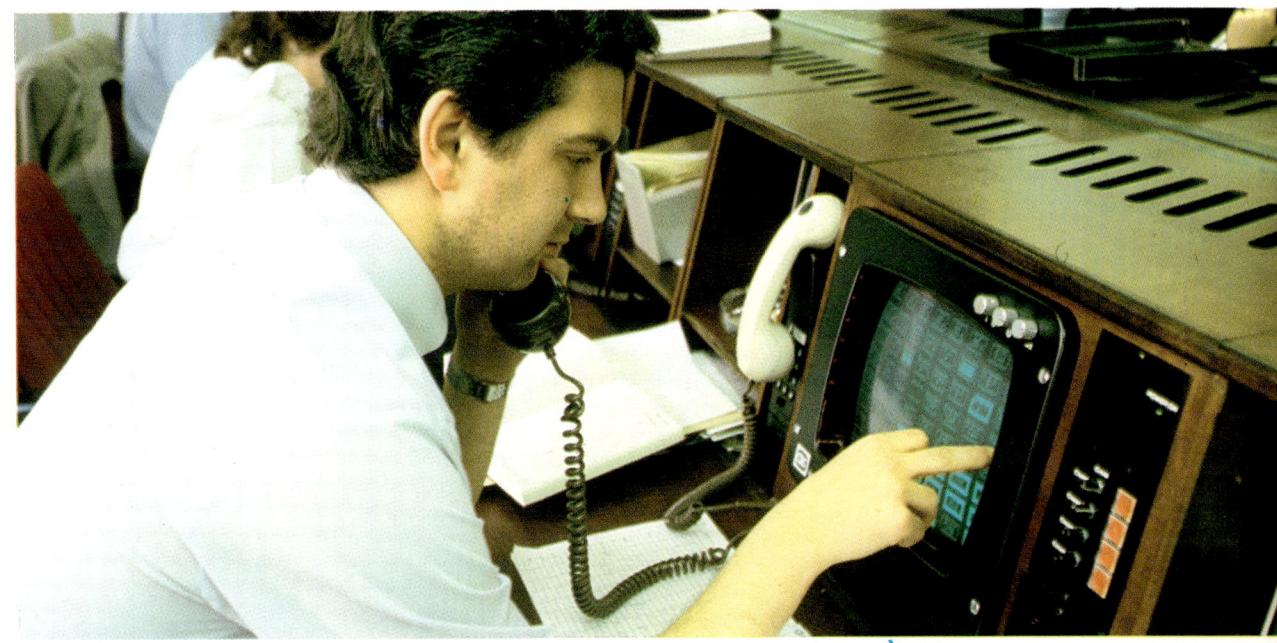

Joysticks and mice

In a similar way, joysticks and push buttons can be used to move arrows around a screen to select options. And, of course, they are also used to control the movement of characters in a game.

Some of the latest business computers use what is called a mouse, a little hand-held pad you move around a table top which at the same time moves a pointer over the screen. You then move the pointer to choose a picture, or "icon" as it is sometimes called, describing what you want to do. If you choose an icon representing a paintbrush, and then press a button on the mouse, you can move the

The cockpit of a Space Shuttle. Shuttle astronauts have several computers on board to monitor the Shuttle's performance.

mouse to draw on the screen. If you then choose an icon showing diagonal lines or spots, your drawing automatically gets shaded in with lines or spots. This mouse and icon method is easy and fun to use. The latest devices are designed to make the computer easy to use, even for someone who is unfamiliar with computers.

Output

However, this is only one side of the story. Computers also have to communicate with us – provide us with "output." The most common method is for the computer to display words on a screen or on paper fed into a printer. Screens are already replacing dials and counters in many branches of engineering, especially in aircraft cockpits. In the future, information will appear less and less as words and numbers and more as diagrams – and in color. Some computers will be able to talk to us. Although screens and printers will continue to be the main way of getting information out, it may become less obvious that computers are involved. For example, sensors and computers could send information to each other, enabling controls such as motors or levers to be altered without any person being involved. New stock could be ordered automatically for stores, for example, and then paid for automatically. In the future, computers will simply do things on their own – which you may consider a frightening thought.

Leisure and learning

In today's world, it is increasingly important to become familiar with computers.

Computers have been in use in schools for some time now, but they have not yet brought about any great changes in education. There are, however, many ways in which computers could help us to learn.

Helping the handicapped

Some of the greatest benefits of computer-aided learning could be experienced by handicapped people. Most of us can communicate with others by writing, talking or drawing, but some handicapped people cannot do so. Computers can provide these people with a means of communication. For example, a computer can enable someone who cannot even hold a pencil to make a drawing. A simple lever can be connected to the computer. Then, using this lever, the person can control a dot on the screen and make it draw straight lines, even if he or she cannot hold the lever steady. The person can also use a push button which, when pressed, makes the dot on the screen draw a circle. In this way a handicapped person can draw pictures for the first time. How exciting that must be!

There is also an experimental program to help handicapped children who cannot speak or hold a pen. The child is provided with a screen, a lever and a push button. On the screen is displayed a whole series of drawings. These may show such objects as a cat, a dog, some people, a

Computer graphics is the term used for the pictures produced by using computers.

Computer games make good use of computer graphics.

house and many other things, including a few words. By moving the lever, the child can control an arrow on the screen and make it point to whichever diagram he or she chooses. Then, by pressing the push button, the child can make the picture appear on a blank area of the screen. The next picture to be chosen is then copied beside it, and so on, so that stories or messages can be built up piece by piece on the screen and later printed on to paper.

Using such a program, or by using a word processor, handicapped people can now be given the all-important chance to communicate.

Unfortunately, such equipment is expensive. This is one area in which computers can play a vital role in helping people, but until more money is made available we shall not be able to give help to everyone who needs it.

LOGO

Computers are, of course, used in schools to teach about computing itself, but they can be used more interestingly to teach pupils about geometry. A special programming language, called LOGO, is used. Using LOGO you can draw shapes on a screen or control simple robots such as turtles, which can scoot around the floor. The interesting thing about LOGO is that it, in effect, puts you (the programmer) where the turtle is, so that commands such as "turn right" and "move forward" are used rather than "move to square number so-and-so."

Small robots, like the turtle, can be programmed to move around and draw pictures.

Computers are used in schools to teach about computing and as aids to learning.

The LOGO language controls the turtle in much the same way that we give people instructions. We might say something like, "Walk down the road and turn right, then go on a bit farther and turn left and there you will find the library." As we give the instructions, we imagine ourselves making the journey. That is how LOGO works, too, so it is easier to learn than some other computer languages.

Using computers in schools

Interesting computer projects have been undertaken by some schools. For example, pupils have produced magazines by using the computer as a word processor. The articles to go into the magazine are entered into the computer using a word processor program. Then they can be edited and printed out on paper. Some schools have linked home computers to other electronic equipment and so picked up data and pictures from weather satellites. In both these examples computers are being used as they are in business and industry – as useful machines rather than as straightforward teaching aids.

What will happen in schools in the future? Somehow computers have not yet had the impact on education that was at first expected. One reason is that there is not enough money available for software and training. Some schools have only one computer, which means, on average, only two minutes "hands-on" computer experience per pupil each week. So it is not really surprising that no great strides have been made. The future for computing in schools depends quite simply on how much money is spent on education.

Students attending a class on computing.

Computers and hobbies

Although personal computers are becoming essential to those with home businesses, some people use them just to play games, and there are also people who use their home computers to pursue their hobbies. For example, there are databases available that can be used to catalog coin collections, or any other kind of collection for that matter. A database can be used to enter, for example, such categories as date, size, a description of the object being collected, or whatever the collector feels is important. The computer can then be used to rearrange the information in various useful ways.

Many people meet computers for the first time in the form of electronic games.

Home computers can also be used to help organize clubs and societies. In this way you can keep a record of the names and addresses of members and dates when subscriptions are due for renewal. In the future, home computers will become increasingly important as a means of storing and arranging information.

Video disks
An important development for the future is the use of a video disk linked to a computer. A video disk can store over 60,000 still pictures (or even clips of film) so it will

be possible, for example, to send for a video disk containing pictures from a famous art gallery. You could use your computer to search through it and put all the pictures of your favorite artist on the screen for you, or pick out something else in any order you choose. Libraries of the future may contain video disks, so that if you wanted to learn about something you could borrow a disk rather than a book.

If, say, you wanted to know about space, you could use your computer to search through the video disk and pick out film clips of the Apollo voyages to the moon, or pictures of Halley's comet, or whatever else you wanted to know. Video disks could well be the encyclopedias of the future.

Video disks are made in ultra-clean rooms.

Artificial intelligence

If a computer beats you at chess, is it really intelligent or has it just followed a large number of simple rules and options?

The answer is that the computer is not really intelligent, for it can only follow the rules with which it has been programmed. However, the time is approaching when computers may be built with the complexity of the human brain, and capable of working much faster. Many scientists now think that there will be computers that have artificial (machine) intelligence.

Before this happens, however, there will have to be important developments in software (the programming of

In NASA's mission operations control room, computers constantly monitor the information sent back during Shuttle flights.

the machines). These programs will have to make the computer capable of judging a situation, working out a plan of action, making decisions and somehow carrying out that plan. These are things we humans do all the time, but to make a computer work this way will take many years of research.

The intelligent computer?

In 1936 a brilliant British mathematician called Alan Turing developed the theory of a universal computer. Later he became involved in making Britain's first electronic

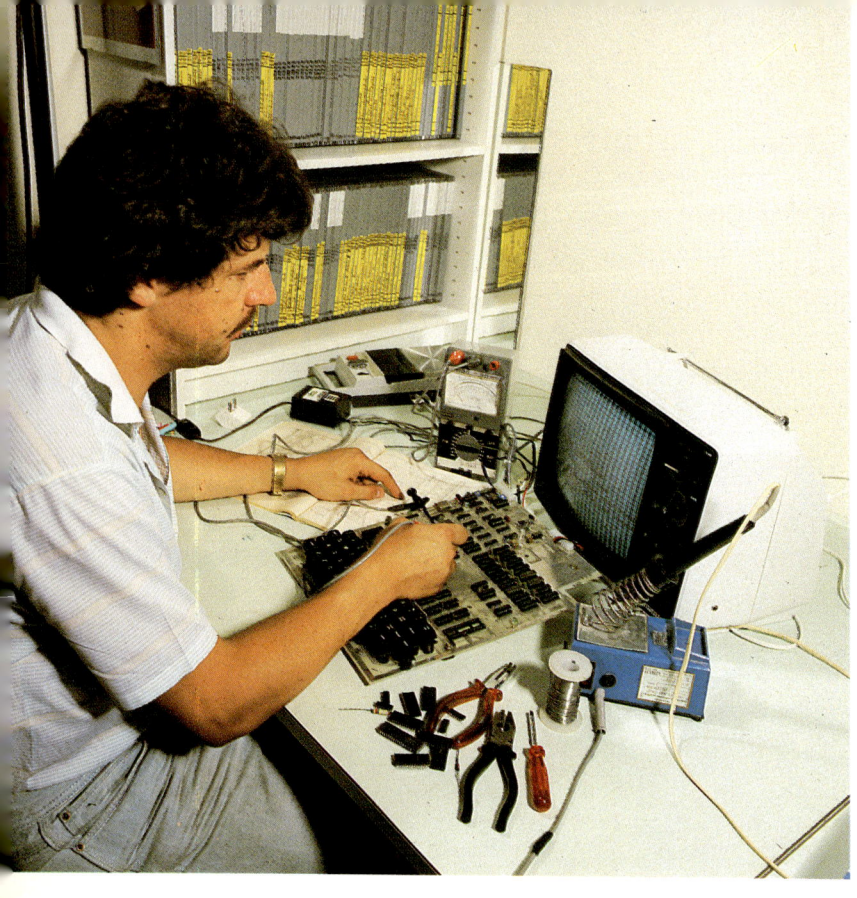

A computer circuit board is tested during a routine maintenance operation.

computer. He suggested a test to show whether or not a computer was intelligent. This was to place a person and the computer out of sight and then get someone else to type out questions and receive answers from either the computer or the person. If it was impossible to tell which replies came from the computer and which from the human, then the computer could be called intelligent. So far no machine has passed the test.

Much research has been done in artificial intelligence. For example, there is a computer program called ELIZA, which can hold a simple conversation with someone by picking up his or her words and matching them to an appropriate reply. You might say "I don't understand computers." ELIZA might reply "I'M SORRY TO HEAR THAT." You say "Yes, I can't get the programs to run." ELIZA might reply "CAN YOU GIVE AN EXAMPLE?" and so on. At first sight the computer seems intelligent, but really it is only picking up key words and giving replies that seem almost human. It cannot introduce any new ideas.

In hospitals, computers are used to store medical records, control equipment and help diagnose illness.

"Expert" computers

There are already "expert" computer systems that have stored in them vast amounts of information about particular subjects. For example, an expert computer system used by doctors can ask a patient questions and match the answers with the best medical knowledge available, which has been programmed into it. In some cases the computer can actually diagnose what is wrong with the patient.

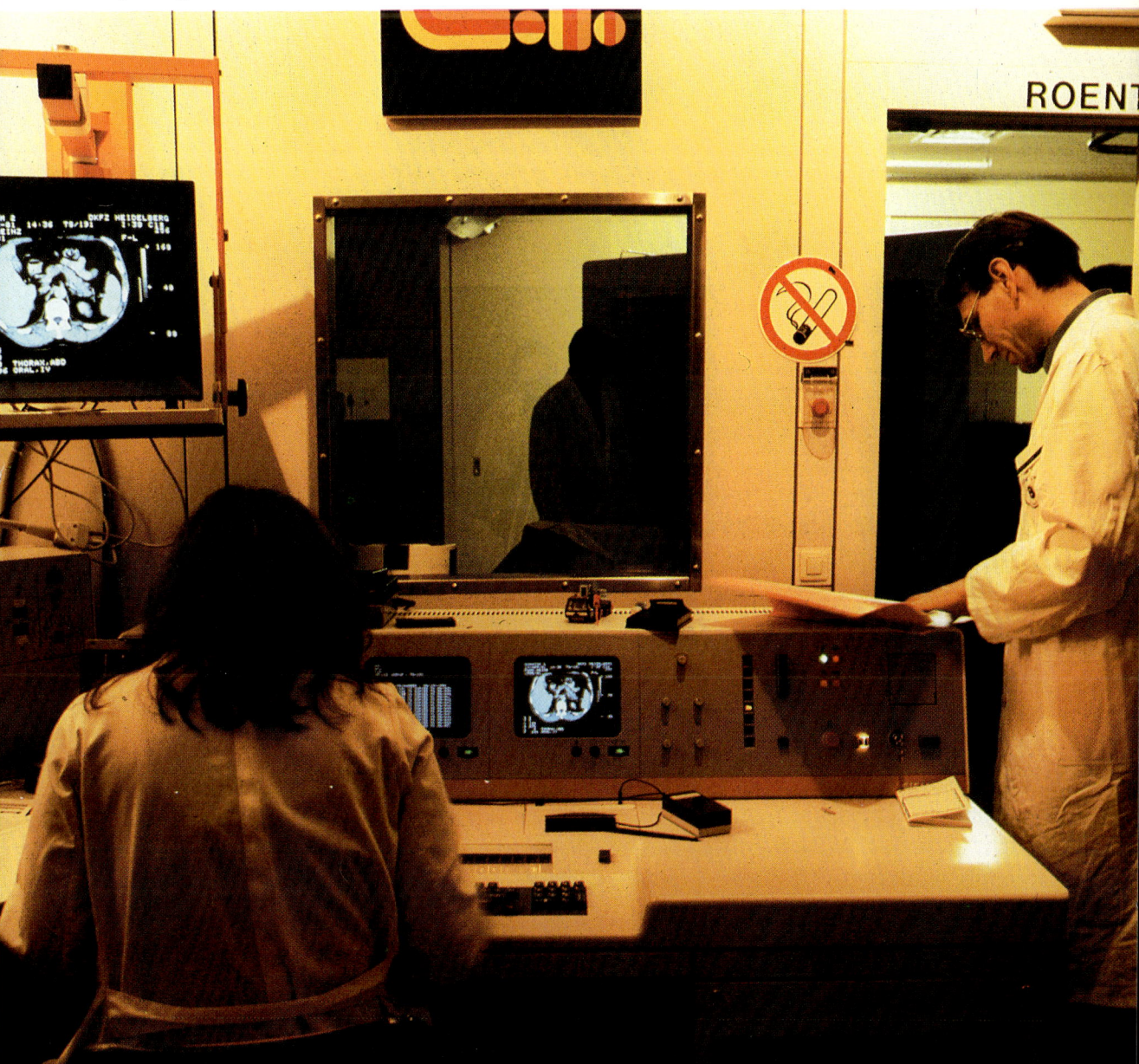

Computers are often used in laboratories to process the results of experiments.

There are also expert computers to help geologists in their search for minerals. Another such expert system contains information about chemical molecules, which it is able to study and identify just as if it were a highly trained human researcher. This is an important step towards developing artificial intelligence.

What the computer *cannot* do at present is tackle a problem that is unlike anything the programmers have thought of. A truly intelligent computer would have to be programmed to learn by its mistakes and through experience, much the way we do, by tackling problems it had never seen before.

Intelligent robots

Developing computers with artificial intelligence is important in robotics. Most robots in use today are not really intelligent, and simply follow set routines. A paint-spraying robot will go on spraying paint into thin air even if the item to be painted does not appear. However, newer robots are being fitted with sensors to provide an input to a computer which can then control what the robot does according to what it sees. The wild paint-spraying robot could then "see" whether or not there was something to be painted, and could take appropriate action.

Although some people argue that a machine cannot ever really be intelligent, there will eventually be many machines that will show intelligent behavior. Such a machine could be linked with several expert systems. This would give it the ability to make decisions based on more information than any one person could ever know.

The idea of intelligent computers worries many people, and there are those who think such machines could present a threat to us and so should not be made. As yet, however, the human brain remains far more complex than any computer we possess.

A robot spraying a car body with paint. It has been "taught" to perform this task and will go on spraying paint even if another car does not appear.

Glossary

Artificial intelligence The kind of intelligence many people believe it will be possible to build into computers of the future. Also called Machine Intelligence.

BASIC Beginner's All-purpose Symbolic Instruction Code, the most popular language used on home computers.

Computer-aided design (CAD) Computer programs that help people in industry to design products, such as cars and other machinery.

Chips Tiny pieces of silicon with complex electrical circuits etched on them.

Data A series of words or numbers, or any information used by a computer.

Database A large store of information held in a computer. This information can be picked up by other computers over a telephone, or by cable.

Hardware The machinery that makes up a computer, without the programs that make it work.

LOGO A programming language originally designed to teach children about mathematics. It can be used to control small mobile robots, or to draw graphics on a screen.

Machine code The language used by the computer itself, made up of a series of 0s and 1s, which are actually electrical impulses. 0 means "off" and 1 means "on."

Microprocessor A chip that is the "brains" of a computer and controls all its operations.

Program A set of instructions given to a computer, written in a special language.

Sensors Devices that take information about the world, turn it into electrical signals, and pass it to a computer to be analyzed.

Software The programs that are fed into the computer equipment to tell it how to work.

Word processor program A program that enables a computer to be used to prepare text. Words can be inserted and deleted, spelling corrected and text rearranged.

Further reading

If you would like to find out more about computers, you may like to read the following books:

Berger, Melvin. *Computers in Your Life.* New York: Harper & Row, 1984.

Freeman, Maryellen and Jeff. *People and Computers.* Akron, OH: Carson-Dellos, 1984.

Greene, Laura. *Computers in Business and Industry.* New York: Franklin Watts, 1984.

Hintz, Martin and Sandra. *Computers in Our World, Today and Tomorrow.* New York: Franklin Watts, 1983.

Lyttle, Richard B. *Computers in the Home.* New York: Franklin Watts, 1984.

The Bookwright Press has produced two complete series on computers. For older readers there is "The Age of Computers" series; all of the books are written by Ian Litterick.

For younger readers there is the "Discovering Computers" series; all of the books are written by Sharon Elliott.

Index

Aircraft 7, 8, 18, 21, 32
Artificial intelligence 41–45

Banks 14, 15

Car industry 23
Colossus 7
Computer-aided design (CAD) 7
Computer crime 17
Concorde 18

Databases 12, 13, 14, 15, 17, 38

Electronics 27
Expert computer systems 43, 44, 45

Factories 18
Flight simulators 7, 8
Ford, Henry 23

Games 6, 38

Home computers 7, 37, 38, 39
Hospitals 13

Icons 31, 32
Industry 7, 10, 18, 23, 24, 26, 27
Information explosion 9
Input 30–32
Internal Revenue Service 14

Japan 18
Joysticks 31

Learning 33, 34, 35
Light pens 31

Magnetic disks 7
Mice 31, 32

Microprocessors 20, 21
Money 11, 15

Output 32

Police 14
Programming languages
    BASIC 28
    ELIZA 42
    LOGO 35, 36, 37

Robots 36, 44, 45

Satellites 37
Schools 33, 37
Sensors 20, 21, 30, 32
Silicon chips 18, 20, 21, 24, 27
Software 37, 41
Speech synthesis 28

Telephones 4
Touch screens 31
Transportation 18
Turing, Alan 41
Turtle 36, 37

Unemployment 24
United States 17, 18
Universal computer 41

Video disks 39, 40

Word processors 11, 35, 37
World War II 7, 24

Acknowledgments

The publisher would like to thank all those who provided pictures on the following pages: British Telecommunications PLC 14, 31; Bruce Coleman Limited 23 (C. Molyneux), 32 (M. Freeman), 34, 38 (D. Austen); Cameraprix-Hutchison 16; PHOTRI 7 (both), 11, 19, 27, 44; Rex Features *cover*, 39; Science Photo Library 15 (H. Morgan), 17 (J. Mason), 36 (P. Aprhamian), 37 (J. Howard); TOPHAM 10, 30, 41; Malcolm S. Walker 4–5, 12–13, 20–21) ZEFA 6, 8, 9, 22, 25, 33, 35, 45, 2–3 (A. Roberts), 26 (K. Benser), 29 & 42 (H. R. Bramaz), 43 (Lorenz).